Alfred's Basic Piano Lib

Prep Course

FOR THE YOUNG BEGINNER

Willard A. Palmer · Morton Manus · Amanda Vick Lethco

Theory Book · Level C

INSTRUCTIONS FOR USE

1. This book is designed for use with Alfred's PREP COURSE for the YOUNG BEGINNER, LESSON BOOK C. The first assignment should be made when the student receives the Lesson Book.

2. Young beginners benefit greatly from supplementary studies, games and puzzles that review all principles previously studied. They also need much reinforcement of new concepts covered in the Lesson Book. To accomplish these goals, this book is coordinated page-by-page with the corresponding Lesson Book, and all assignments should be made according to the instructions in the upper right corner of each page of the THEORY BOOK.

3. Piano students are especially in need of additional rhythm drills, along with studies that improve musicianship. The use of "dynamic clapping," coupled with the experience of conducting music using a pencil or baton (a concept introduced in THEORY BOOK B), ensures progress in these areas.

4. All students must be able to recognize immediately the proper hand position to be used to play music written in any five-finger position. Other methods, we believe, have generally failed to deal adequately with the development of this skill; this book contains studies that should remedy this problem.

5. Private students are usually expected to complete theory assignments at home, with the written work checked at the beginning of each lesson or before the next assignment is made. Some of the rhythm exercises, particularly those involving "dynamic clapping," will need the supervision of the teacher, however.

6. In class teaching, the theory assignments are often used as classroom drill, completed at the lesson.

Illustrations by Christine Finn · Music Engraving by Nancy Butler

Use with ALFRED'S PREP COURSE,
Lesson Book C, page 4.

Review

1. Draw a BRACE and a BAR LINE at the beginning of the two staffs below, joining them together to make one GRAND STAFF.

2. Draw a TREBLE or G CLEF SIGN at the beginning of the upper staff.

3. Draw a BASS or F CLEF SIGN at the beginning of the lower staff.

4. Draw a DOUBLE BAR with REPEAT SIGNS at the end of the grand staff.

5. Use 3 more BAR LINES to divide the grand staff into 4 measures.

NOTES YOU HAVE LEARNED

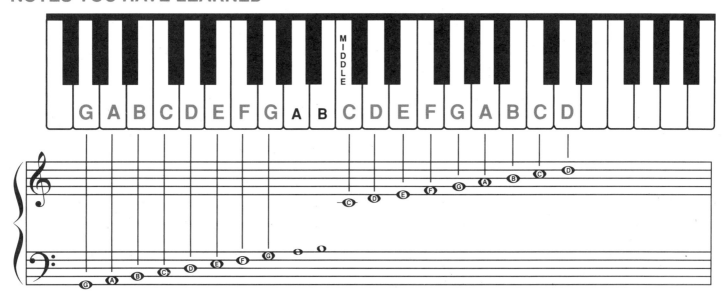

6. Write the names of the notes in the boxes.

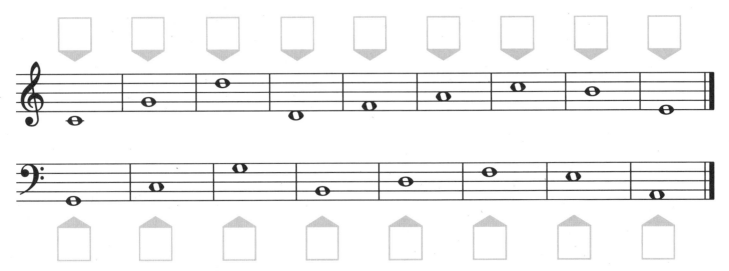

Use with page 4.

Bass Clef and Treble Clef Word-Matching

The notes in each box spell a word.

1. Write the name of each note in the space below it.
2. Draw lines connecting the dots on the boxes in which the same words are spelled.

Score 20 for each pair of boxes correctly connected.

PERFECT SCORE = 140

YOUR SCORE: _____

Review

Use with page 5.

TIME SIGNATURE

$\frac{4}{4}$ means **4** beats to each measure.

$\frac{4}{4}$ a **QUARTER NOTE** ♩ gets 1 beat.

	NOTE	REST	COUNT	TOTAL NUMBER OF COUNTS
QUARTER	♩	𝄽	"1"	1
HALF	♩	▬	"1 - 2"	2
WHOLE	𝅝	▬	"1 - 2 - 3 - 4"	4

1. In the top box under each note, write the number of counts the note receives.

2. In the bottom box draw the rest that receives the same value, as shown in the first example.

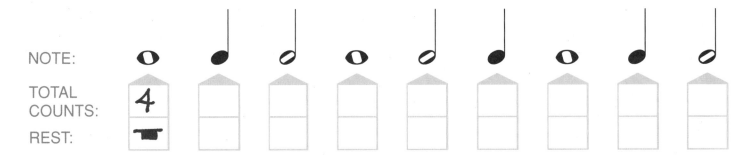

NOTE:

TOTAL COUNTS: **4**

REST:

BAR LINES divide the music into MEASURES. Each measure in $\frac{4}{4}$ time has notes adding up to 4 counts.

3. Complete each measure by adding just one **G** to each, so the counts in each add up to 4:

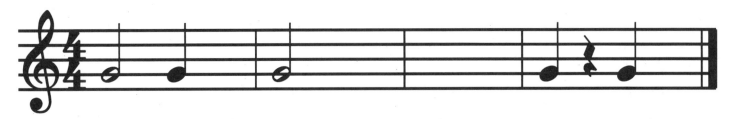

4. Complete each measure by adding just one **F** to each, so the counts in each add up to 4:

Dynamic Clapping

1. Fill in the blanks below with dynamic signs that mean the same as the words below the blanks.

2. Clap once for each note, counting aloud. Carefully observe all the dynamic signs you have written. Clap and count softly in the soft measures, loudly in the loud measures, etc.
Observe all repeat signs.

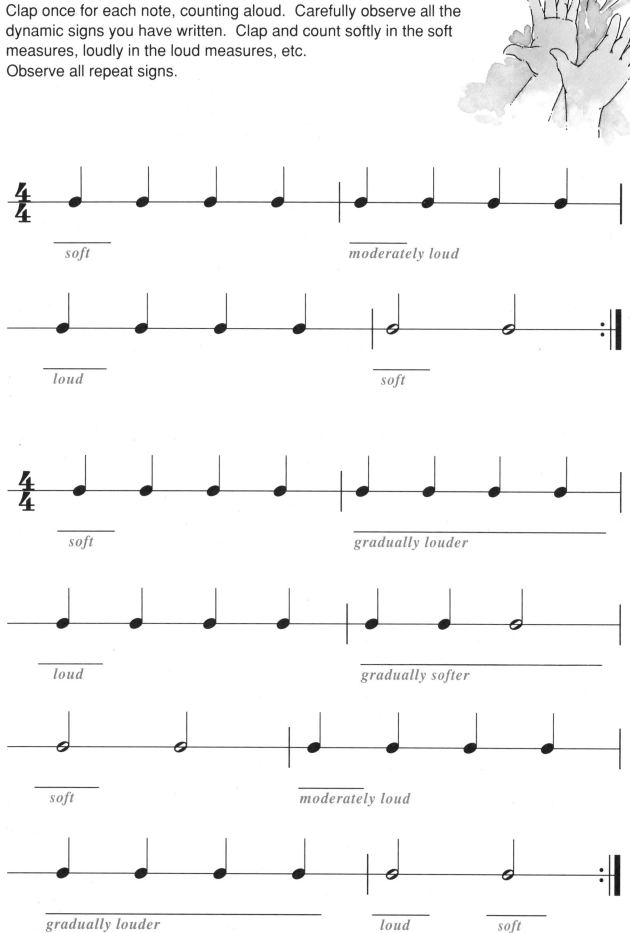

Reviewing C Position

Use with page 6.

Pat's Cat's Hat

1. Draw bar lines to divide the music into measures. Use a DOUBLE BAR at the end of the piece.
2. Write the names of the notes in the boxes.
3. Play the music.

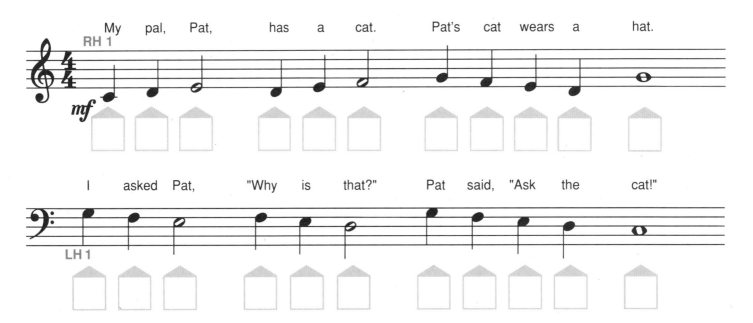

Spelling with Notes

4. Write the notes that spell these words. Use QUARTER, HALF, or WHOLE notes so the notes in each measure add up to 4 counts.

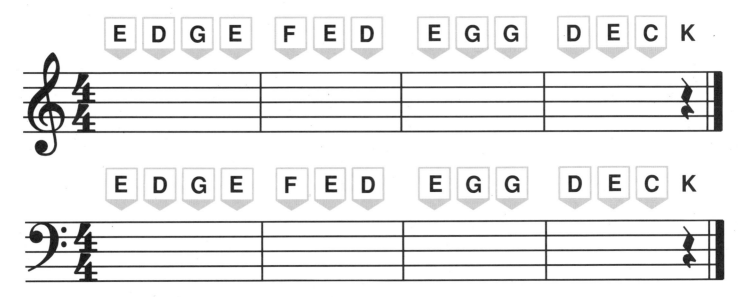

Reviewing Melodic Intervals in C Position

Distances between tones are measured in INTERVALS. Notes played SEPARATELY make MELODIC INTERVALS.

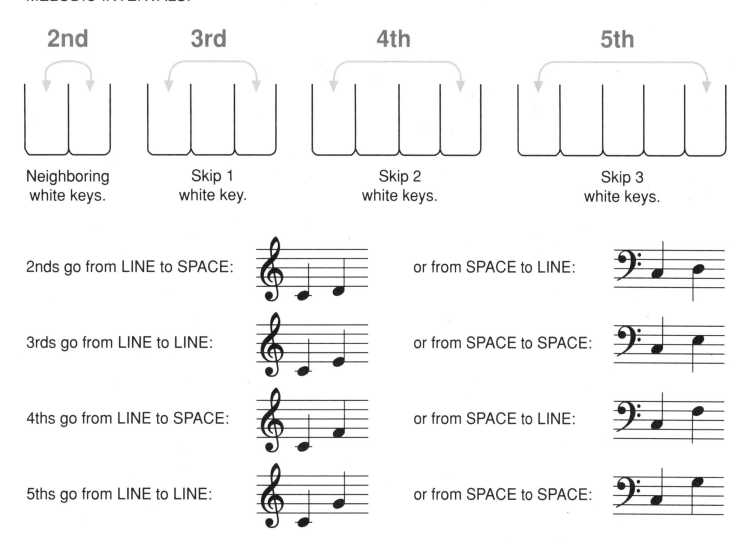

Identify the intervals below. If the interval moves UP, write "UP" in the top box. If it moves DOWN, write "DOWN" in the top box. If the note does not move up or down, write "SAME NOTE."

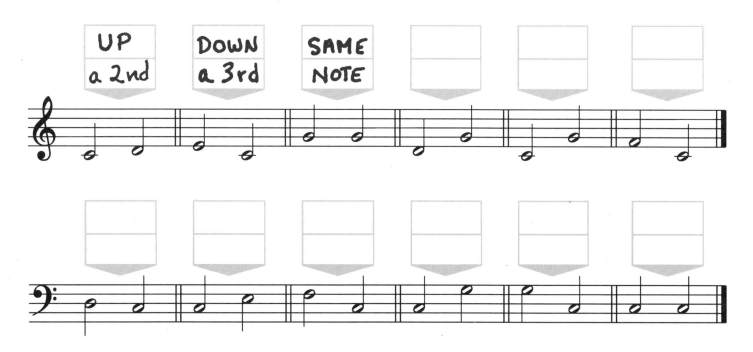

Use with page 7.

Reviewing ¾ Time

3/4 means **3** beats to each measure.
a **QUARTER NOTE** ♩ gets 1 beat.

♩. = DOTTED HALF NOTE
COUNT: "1 - 2 - 3"

1. Draw BAR LINES through the treble and bass staffs, to divide the following music into measures. Use a DOUBLE BAR at the end of the last line.
2. Add TIES between the last two notes of the first, third and fourth lines.
3. Add a WHOLE REST in each measure of the BASS STAFF when the LH is not playing, and in the TREBLE STAFF when the RH is not playing.
   The WHOLE REST should hang down from the fourth line of the staff:
4. Play, counting aloud.

Beautiful Brown Eyes

Moderately fast

Reviewing Harmonic Intervals in C Position

Notes played together make **HARMONIC INTERVALS.**

1. Play these HARMONIC INTERVALS, saying the names aloud:

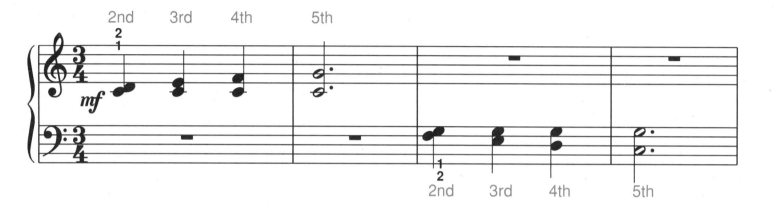

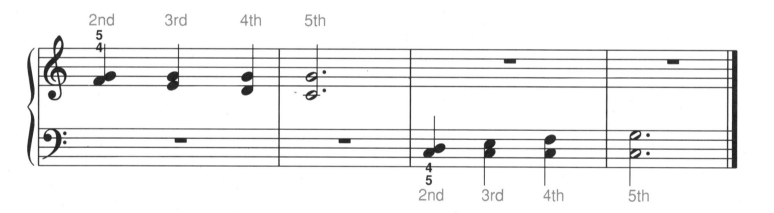

2. In the upper boxes, write the names of the notes that complete these HARMONIC INTERVALS:

2nd ⟨ ☐ / C

2nd ⟨ ☐ / D

2nd ⟨ ☐ / E

2nd ⟨ ☐ / F

3rd ⟨ ☐ / C

3rd ⟨ ☐ / D

3rd ⟨ ☐ / E

4th ⟨ ☐ / C

4th ⟨ ☐ / D

5th ⟨ ☐ / C

Use with pages 8 & 9.

Reviewing the Sharp Sign

The **SHARP SIGN** before a note means play the next key to the right, whether black or white!

1. Write the names of the ♯ keys in the boxes:

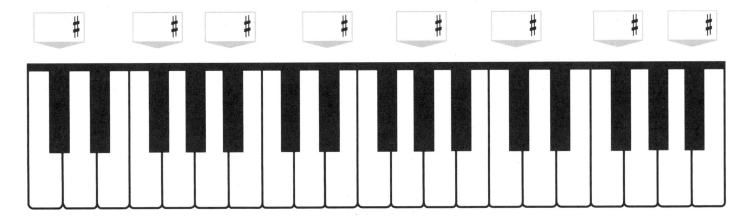

2. Some sharps are WHITE KEYS. The next key to the right of E is a white key, and the next key to the right of B is a white key. This means that F may also be called E♯, and C may also be called B♯.

   Write two NAMES for each key in the boxes above it.

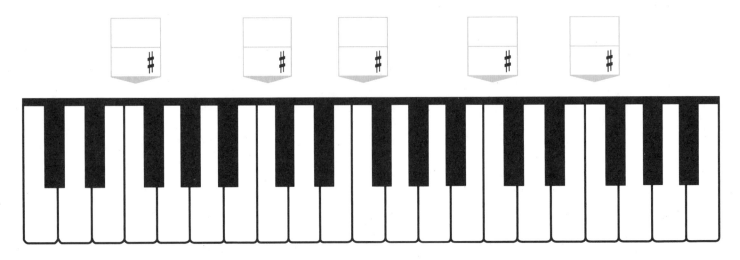

Use with pages 8 & 9.

A Sharp Song

This song is very easy, and fun to play!
Only BLACK KEYS are used, and only third fingers are used.

LH 3 is used ONLY on the F♯ ABOVE MIDDLE C.
RH 3 plays all other keys, CROSSING OVER the LH to play keys below the LH F♯.

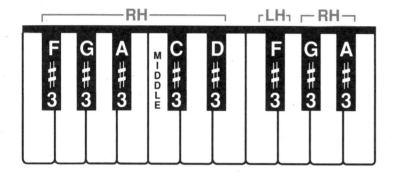

REMEMBER!
The SHARP SIGN before a note applies to that note each time it appears in the same measure!

1. In the first measure below, is the fourth note a sharp note? Answer: _____
2. Write the names of the notes in the boxes.
3. Play and say the note names: "**A** SHARP," etc.

STEMS UP = RH   STEMS DOWN = LH

Moderately slow

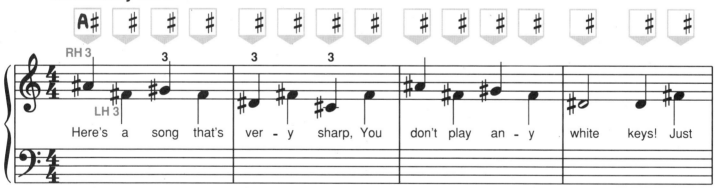

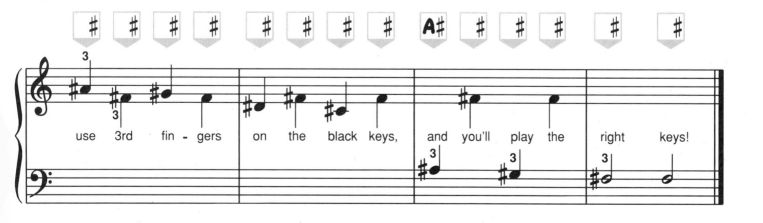

Use with page 10.

Reviewing G Position

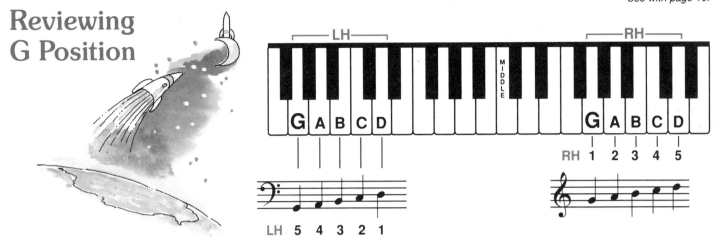

Up to the Moon

1. Add bar lines to divide the music into measures. Use a DOUBLE BAR at the end.
2. Write the names of the notes in the boxes.　　3. Play.

Spelling with Notes

4. Write the notes from the G POSITION that spell these words. Use QUARTER, HALF, DOTTED HALF or WHOLE notes so the notes in each measure add up to 4 counts.

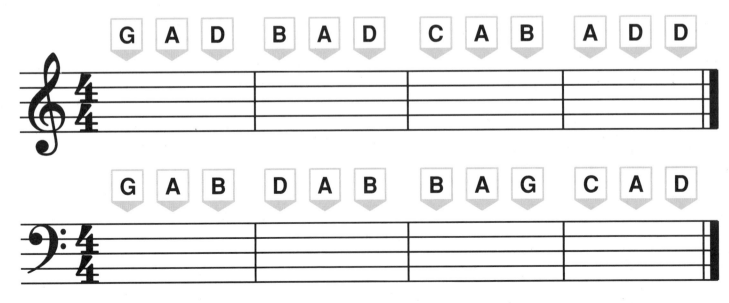

Reviewing Melodic Intervals in G Position

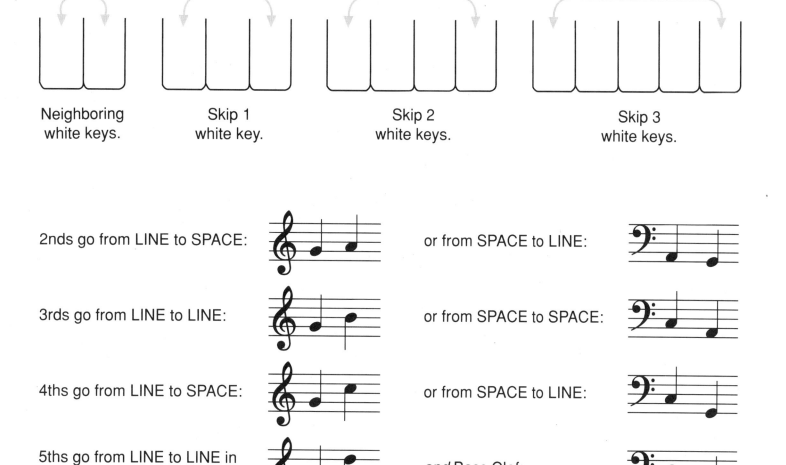

2nd
Neighboring white keys.

3rd
Skip 1 white key.

4th
Skip 2 white keys.

5th
Skip 3 white keys.

2nds go from LINE to SPACE: or from SPACE to LINE:

3rds go from LINE to LINE: or from SPACE to SPACE:

4ths go from LINE to SPACE: or from SPACE to LINE:

5ths go from LINE to LINE in
G Position in Treble Clef: *and* Bass Clef:

Identify the intervals below. If the interval moves UP, write "UP" in the top box. If it moves DOWN, write "DOWN" in the top box. If the note does not move up or down, write "SAME NOTE."

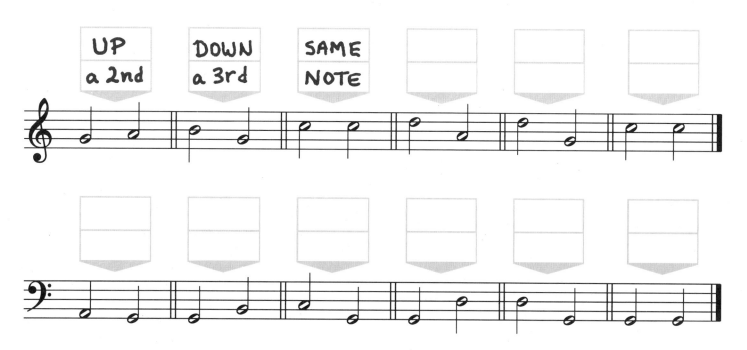

UP
a 2nd

DOWN
a 3rd

SAME
NOTE

Reviewing Staccato

Use with pages 12 & 13.

STACCATO is indicated by a DOT over or under the note.
Release each staccato note instantly.

1. Add a STACCATO DOT to each of the following notes. If the note stem points
   DOWN, put the dot OVER the note. If the stem points UP, put the dot UNDER the note.
2. Play.

Moderately

2nd time play both hands ONE OCTAVE (8 notes) higher.

mf What goes | hop, hop, hop? | Kan - ga - roos and | rab - bits do.

What else goes | hop, hop, hop? | Some - times you and | I do, too!

The Accent Sign >

When there is an ACCENT SIGN over or under a note, play that note LOUDER.

1. Draw an accent sign > under each BASS note.
2. Play.

March

2nd time play both hands ONE OCTAVE lower.

mf If I had a | big bass drum, | I'd play ac - cents | Boom! Boom! Boom!

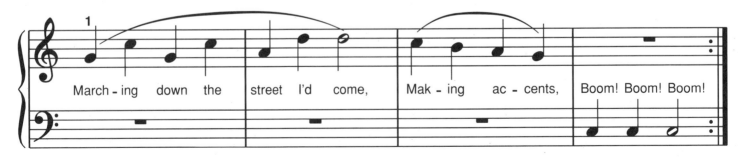

March - ing down the | street I'd come, | Mak - ing ac - cents, | Boom! Boom! Boom!

Reviewing Harmonic Intervals in G Position

1. Play these HARMONIC INTERVALS, saying the names aloud:

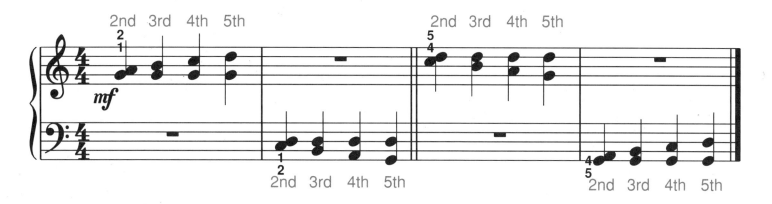

2. In the upper boxes, write the names of the notes that complete these HARMONIC INTERVALS:

2nd < [ ] / G   **2nd** < [ ] / A   **2nd** < [ ] / B   **2nd** < [ ] / C   **3rd** < [ ] / G

3rd < [ ] / A   **3rd** < [ ] / B   **4th** < [ ] / G   **4th** < [ ] / A   **5th** < [ ] / G

Reviewing Slurs, Phrases, Legato

A **SLUR** over or under a group of notes means they are played **LEGATO** (smoothly connected).

SLURS often divide the music into **PHRASES** (musical thoughts or sentences).
Notice how the following slurs separate the question from the answer, and at the same time show that they are played LEGATO:

Play the above line of music.

• Be sure to play LEGATO.

• Lift at the end of each phrase, just after you count "1 - 2 - 3 - 4" for the whole notes.
   This lift should be like taking a slight breath at the end of the question and at the end of the answer, without adding any time to the value of the notes.

Reviewing the Flat Sign

The **FLAT SIGN** before a note means play the next key to the LEFT, whether black or white!

1. Write the names of the ♭ keys in the boxes:

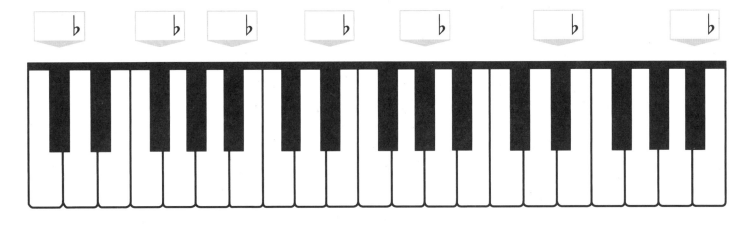

2. Some flats are WHITE KEYS. The next key to the left of C is a white key, and the next key to the left of F is a white key. This means that B may also be called C♭, and E may also be called F♭.

Write two NAMES for each key in the boxes above it.

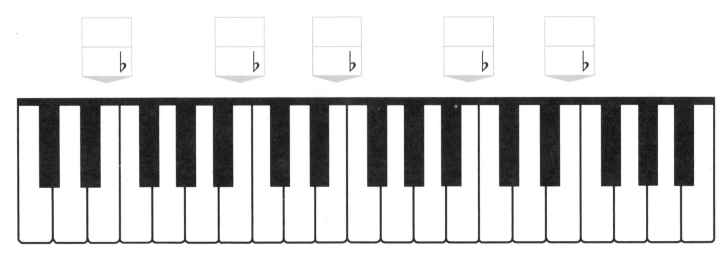

Our Car Has 5 Flats

This piece uses BLACK KEYS ONLY.
Place LH 4 3 2 on G♭, A♭ and B♭. Place RH 2 3 on D♭ and E♭.

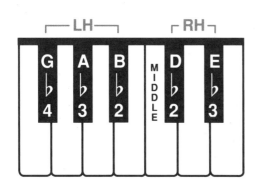

REMEMBER!

The FLAT SIGN before a note applies to that note each time it appears in the same measure!

1. Write the names of the notes in the boxes.
2. Play and say the note names: "G FLAT," etc.

Each Black Key has Two Names!

Use with page 14.

Each black key is the ♯ of the white key to its LEFT.
It is also called the ♭ of the white key to its RIGHT.

1. Fill in the boxes with both names of the indicated black keys, as shown in the example.

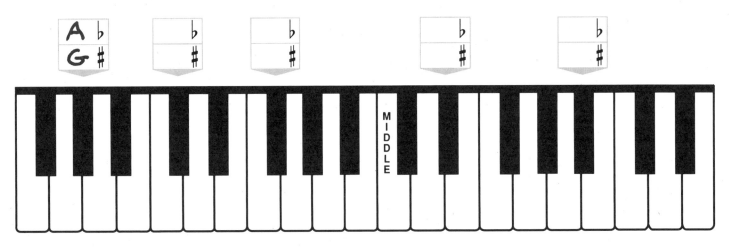

White Keys with Two Names

You have learned that some flats and sharps can be white keys.

2. Fill in the boxes with the ♯ or ♭ name of the indicated white keys, as shown in the example.

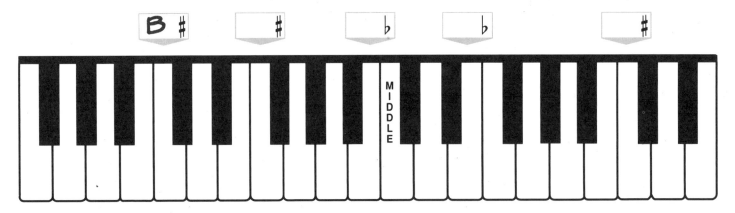

When two DIFFERENT notes are used for the SAME KEY, they are called ENHARMONIC NOTES.

3. Write an ENHARMONIC NOTE after each note on the staffs below, as shown in the example.
   Use half notes to complete each measure.

Incomplete Measure

When a piece begins with an INCOMPLETE MEASURE, the missing counts are found in the LAST MEASURE.

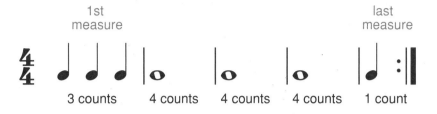

When you repeat the piece, you will have exactly one COMPLETE measure when you go from the LAST measure to the FIRST measure!

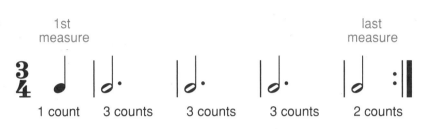

1. In each of these *PONY SONGS* the last note is missing.
   The name of the missing note is in the box above the measure.
   Add the note, giving it its proper value.
2. Write the note names in the empty boxes,
   then play both *SONGS*, counting aloud.

Pony Song No. 1

Moderately fast

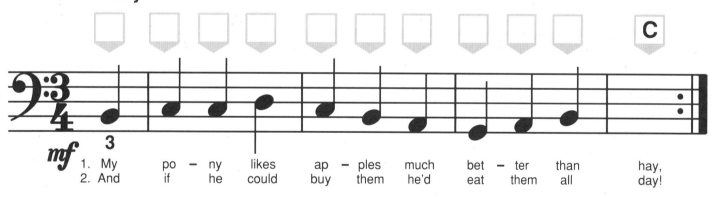

1. My po – ny likes ap – ples much bet – ter than hay,
2. And if he could buy them he'd eat them all day!

Pony Song No. 2

Moderately fast

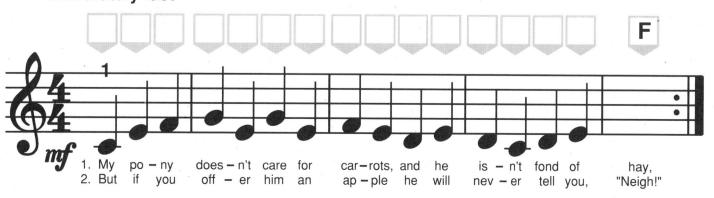

1. My po – ny does – n't care for car – rots, and he is – n't fond of hay,
2. But if you off – er him an ap – ple he will nev – er tell you, "Neigh!"

Use with pages 16 & 17.

More Incomplete Measures

Each of the following examples begins with an INCOMPLETE MEASURE.

1. Answer the questions below each example.
    Pay very close attention to the TIME SIGNATURES. Remember that the last measure must contain only the number of counts that are missing in the first (incomplete) measure!

How many counts are there in the first (incomplete) measure above? _____

How many counts should there be in the last measure? _____

How many counts are there in the first (incomplete) measure above? _____

How many counts should there be in the last measure? _____

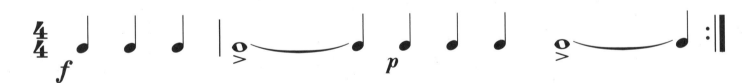

How many counts are there in the first (incomplete) measure above? _____

How many counts should there be in the last measure? _____

2. Add the missing bar lines to each of the above examples.
    Does the number of counts in the last measure of each example agree with the answer you gave?

3. CLAP and COUNT each of the above examples.
    Use DYNAMIC CLAPPING: clap and count loudly and softly, as indicated by the DYNAMIC SIGNS.

    Notice that each example is REPEATED. There should be no pause in clapping or counting when you go from the last measure back to the beginning.

Reading in Middle C Position

The Ski Lift

1. Write the names of the notes in the boxes.
2. Play, saying the note names aloud.

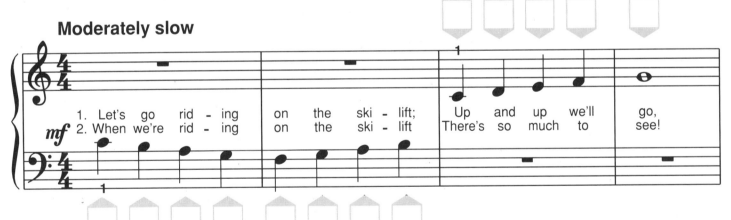

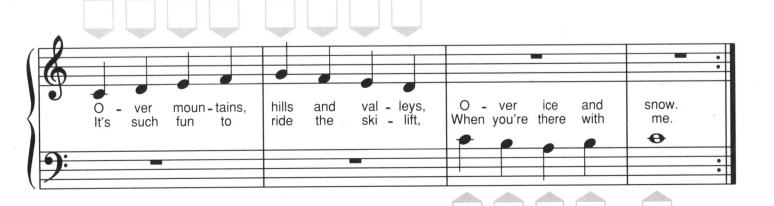

22

Use with pages 18 & 19.

Middle C Position ∾ *Right-Side-Up Quiz*

Write the name of each note in the square BELOW THE NOTE.
Ignore the upside-down clef sign on the right side of each staff.

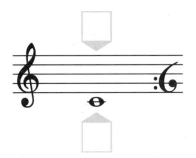

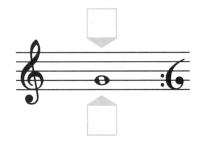

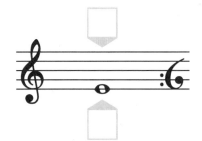

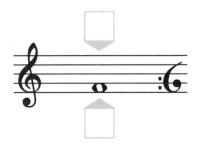

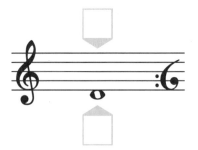

IMPORTANT! Turn the book upside down and complete this page again.

Ignore the upside-down clef sign on the right side of each staff.
Write the name of each note in the square BELOW THE NOTE.

Middle C Position ∾ *Upside-Down Quiz*

Review

Bass-Word Puzzle

ACROSS

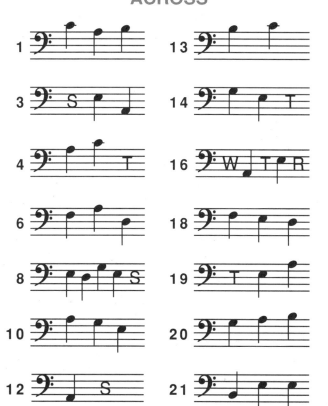

DOWN

Use with pages 22–23.

Review

Treble-Word Puzzle

ACROSS

DOWN

Treble and Bass Clef

Word-Matching Game

Each word in the left column is spelled in the BASS CLEF in the middle column and in the TREBLE CLEF in the right column.

Write the number of each word in the matching space before the notes in the BASS and TREBLE columns.

1. **EDGE**

2. **BAG**

3. **FACE**

4. **FEED**

5. **CAFE**

6. **BEAD**

7. **GAB**

8. **FADE**

9. **DEAF**

10. **BABE**

SCORE 5 for each blank correctly filled.
PERFECT SCORE = 100

YOUR SCORE: _____

Fermatas Are to Hold!

A note or rest over or under a FERMATA ⌒ or ⌣
is held LONGER than its value.

OVER a note, it looks like this:

UNDER a note, it looks like this:

1. Write the names of the notes in the boxes below.
2. Play. Hold the notes with the fermatas
   longer than their values.
3. Play and say or sing the words.
4. How many fermata signs are in this piece? _____

Moderately slow

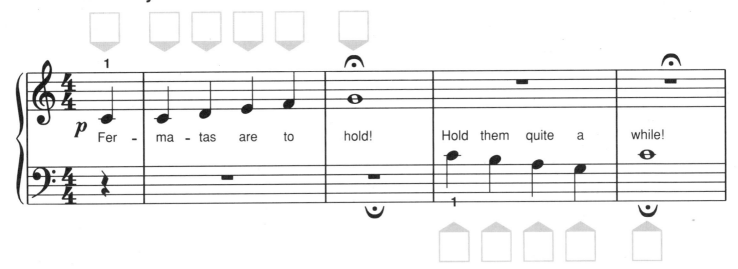

Fer - ma - tas are to hold! Hold them quite a while!

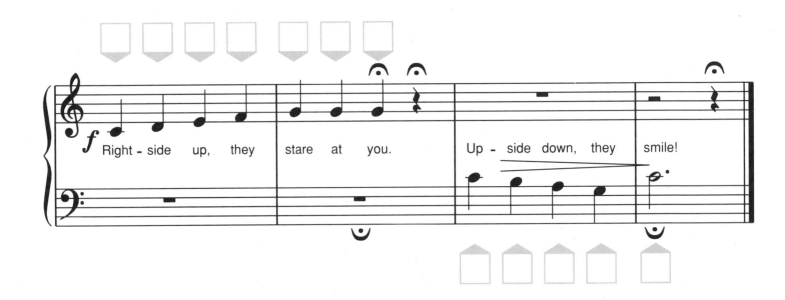

Right - side up, they stare at you. Up - side down, they smile!

Eighth Notes

ONE QUARTER   **TWO EIGHTHS**

EIGHTH NOTES are usually played in PAIRS. They are joined together with a BEAM:

1. Change these quarter notes to EIGHTH NOTES by adding a BEAM to each pair:

> To count music containing eighth notes, divide each beat into 2 parts:
>   count: "one-and" or "quar-ter" for each quarter note;
>   count: "one-and" or "two-8ths" for each pair of eighth notes.

2. Play the following while you count aloud: "One-and, one-and," etc.
    Play again, counting "Quar-ter, quar-ter," etc.

MIDDLE C POSITION

Moderato

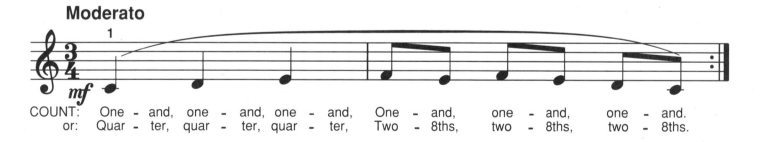

COUNT: One - and, one - and, one - and, One - and, one - and, one - and.
or: Quar - ter, quar - ter, quar - ter, Two - 8ths, two - 8ths, two - 8ths.

COUNT: One - and, one - and, one - and, One - and, one - and, one - and.
or: Quar - ter, quar - ter, quar - ter, Two - 8ths, two - 8ths, two - 8ths.

Use with page 29.

More about Eighths

1. On each of the lines on the right, write ONE NOTE equal to the total value of the eighth notes on the left.

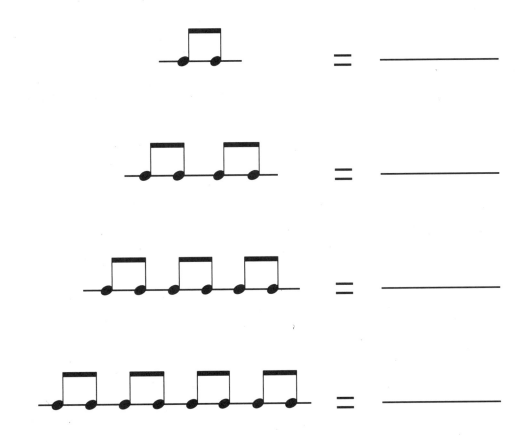

2. Write TWO FULL MEASURES of eighth notes on each of the following lines. Group the eighth notes in PAIRS.

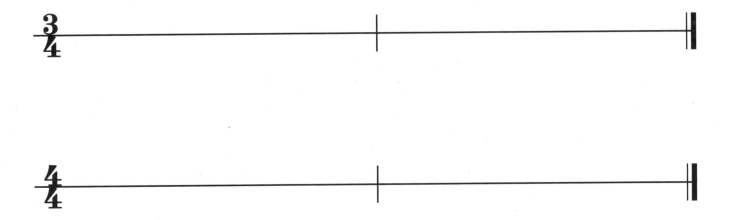

SCORE 20 for each correct answer.
PERFECT SCORE = 120

YOUR SCORE: _____

Try, Try Again!

1. Add the missing bar lines.
2. Add one rest in each measure for the hand that doesn't play.
3. Play and count.

Moderately fast

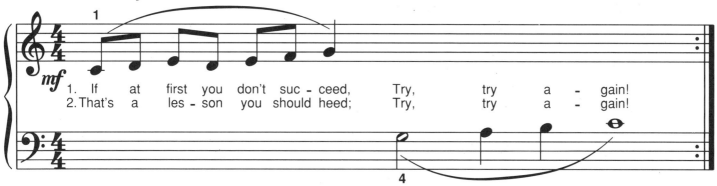

1. If at first you don't suc-ceed, Try, try a-gain!
2. That's a les-son you should heed; Try, try a-gain!

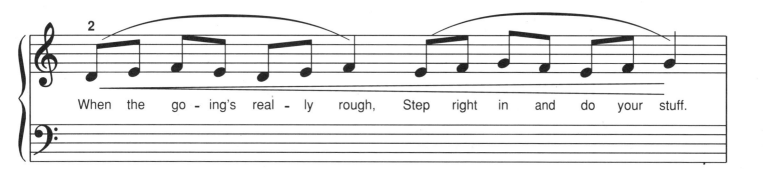

When the go-ing's real-ly rough, Step right in and do your stuff.

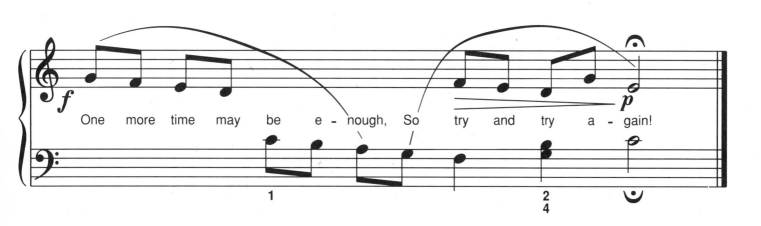

One more time may be e-nough, So try and try a-gain!

Use with pages 32–33.

The Eighth Rest

This is an **EIGHTH REST**.
It means REST FOR THE VALUE OF AN EIGHTH NOTE.

Pairs of EIGHTH NOTES are joined with a beam: or

Single EIGHTH NOTES have a FLAG instead of a beam: or

1. Make the following quarter notes into SINGLE EIGHTH NOTES. Trace the flag, then add flags to the other notes.

2. Trace the first EIGHTH REST, then draw an eighth rest after each of the other eighth notes.

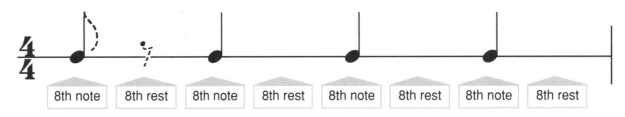

| 8th note | 8th rest | 8th note | 8th rest | 8th note | 8th rest | 8th note | 8th rest |

Reviewing Note & Rest Values

EIGHTH NOTE = ♪   QUARTER NOTE = ♩   HALF NOTE = ♩   WHOLE NOTE = o

EIGHTH REST = 𝄾   QUARTER REST = 𝄽   HALF REST = ▬
(sits on line)   WHOLE REST = ▬
(hangs down)

A WHOLE REST is used to indicate silence for any WHOLE MEASURE of $\frac{3}{4}$ or $\frac{4}{4}$!

3. Complete these measures by adding only ONE REST to each measure:

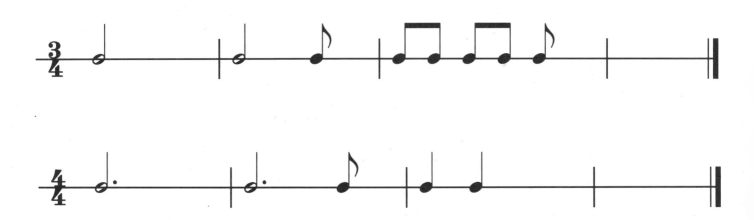

4/4 Rhythms, Using Eighth Notes & Eighth Rests

1. Add the missing bar lines. Use a DOUBLE BAR with a REPEAT SIGN at the end of each line.

2. Count and clap the rhythms. Use DYNAMIC CLAPPING.
   Count "1 & 2 & 3 & 4 &" or "two-eighths, two-eighths, two-eighths" for each measure.

Use with pages 34–35.

A New Time Signature

> **2/4** means **2** beats to each measure.
>
> means a **quarter note** gets 1 beat.

In music, a natural stress or EMPHASIS can be felt on the first beat of each measure.

Say the words to the following measures. Can you tell that they are in **2/4** time?

Sim - ple   Si - mon   met   a   pie - man.

Rain,   rain,   go   a - way!

Directing **2/4** Time

2/4 TIME:

BEGIN HERE   2   END HERE

1

1. Trace these **2/4** patterns with a pencil.

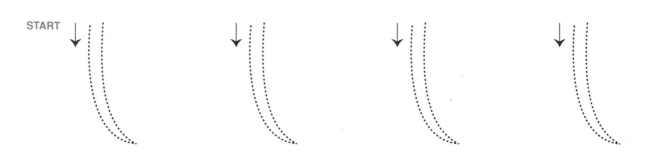

START

2. Using your pencil as a baton, make the **2/4** pattern in the air.

3. Conduct each of the above lines of music, saying the words aloud.

Kookaburra

1. Add bar lines.

2. Play. Observe the accent sign >,
   which means play that one note or chord LOUDER.

Moderately fast

A whole rest is used to indicate
a whole measure of silence in $\frac{2}{4}$ time.

Koo - ka - bur - ra   sits   on   an   old   gum   tree,   Mer - ry, mer - ry

king   of   the   bush   is   he,   Laugh,   Koo - ka - bur - ra,

Laugh,   Koo - ka - bur - ra,   Gay   your   life   must   be!   Whee!

Use with pages 36–37.

Incomplete Measures
Beginning with Eighth Notes

1. Add ONE NOTE or ONE REST to complete each of these lines of music.

   REMEMBER: The last measure must contain only enough counts to complete the first (incomplete) measure.

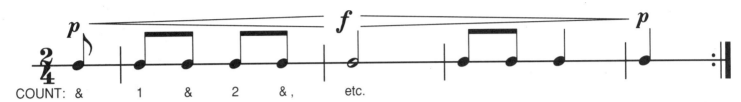

COUNT: &   1   &   2   & ,   etc.

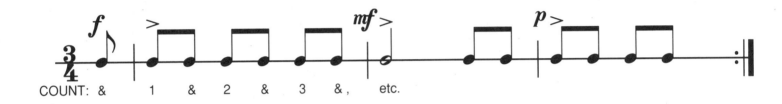

COUNT: &   1   &   2   &   3   & ,   etc.

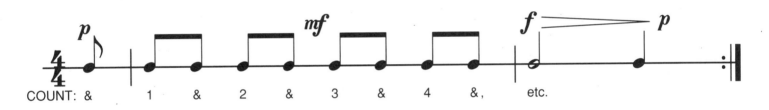

COUNT: &   1   &   2   &   3   &   4   & ,   etc.

2. COUNT and CLAP each of the above examples. Use DYNAMIC CLAPPING.

   Observe the repeat signs, proceeding from the last measure back to the beginning of each line without hesitation.

Rhythm-e-tic

Fill in the blanks with the TOTAL NUMBER OF COUNTS in each example:

 = _____ COUNTS

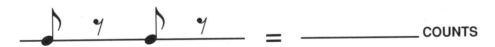 = _____ COUNTS

 = _____ COUNTS

Rhythm Review

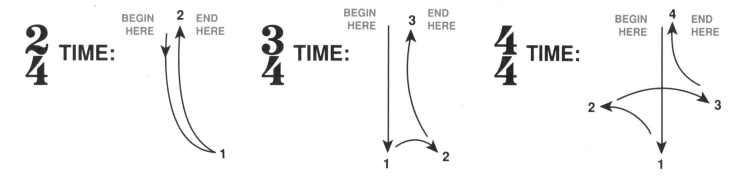

> Notice that the first count of each measure is always a DOWN beat, and the last count of each measure is always an UP beat. This is true in ANY time signature!

1. Using a pencil as a baton, make each of the above patterns in the air several times, counting aloud.
2. Conduct each of the following lines, saying the words aloud.

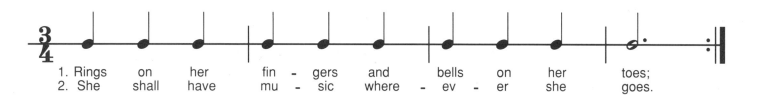

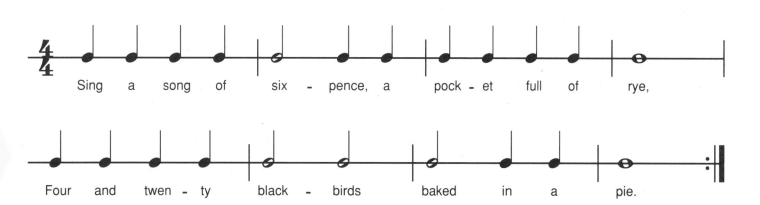

Use with pages 40–41.

More Rhythm Review

1. Say the words of the first line below, clapping ONCE FOR EACH COUNT.

2. Decide whether the words of the line fit best with $\frac{2}{4}$, $\frac{3}{4}$, or $\frac{4}{4}$ time, then add the TIME SIGNATURE and BAR LINES.

3. Proceed to the next line, etc.

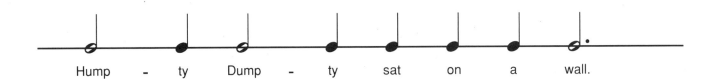

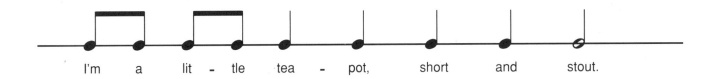

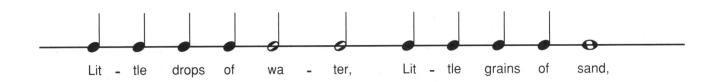

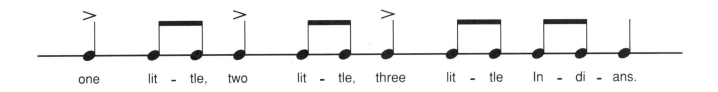

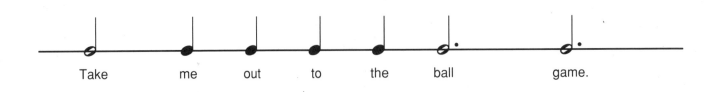

4. Conduct each of the above lines, saying the words aloud.

Recognizing Hand Positions

You have played in three 5-finger positions: C, G, and MIDDLE C.

It is very easy to instantly recognize these positions on the bass and treble staffs.
You can identify the position of the RH or LH if you know just ONE NOTE and
ONE FINGER NUMBER for each hand in each position.

Note that in MIDDLE C POSITION, LH 5 is on F!

A Song without Words (in 3 Positions)

Use with pages 42–43.

This piece uses all three of the positions you have learned. The two quarter rests at the end of each of the first three lines will give you plenty of time to change positions with both hands.

1. Write the names of the notes in the squares.

2. Add fingering to the first LH note and the first RH notes in each position.

3. PLAY, observing all dynamic signs.

Recognizing Hand Positions, continued

Write the name of the 5-finger position in the box following each of these examples.

MIDDLE C POSITION may be abbreviated MC.

REMEMBER! **RH** C POSITION and MC POSITION are the same.
In these cases, either answer will be correct.

LH C POSITION and MC POSITION are NOT the same.

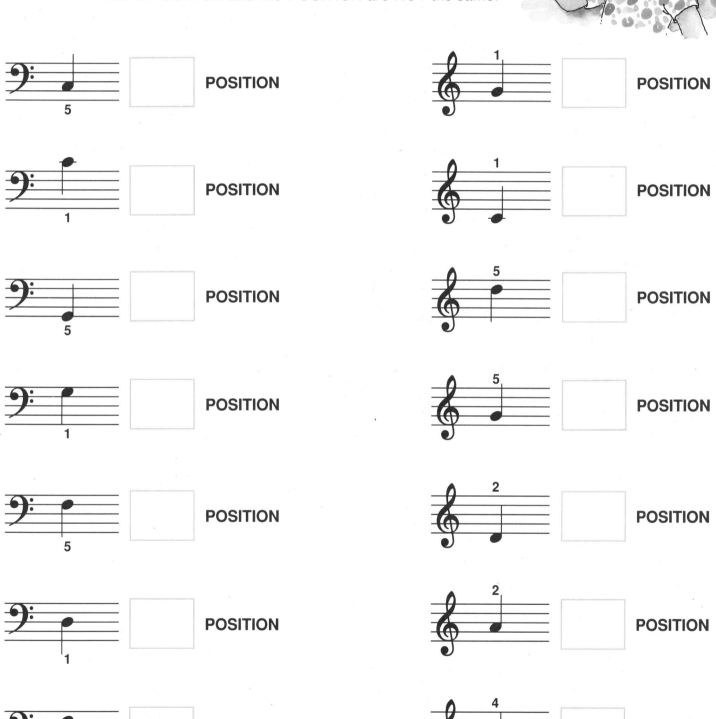

SCORE 10 for each correct answer.

Perfect score = 140

YOUR SCORE: _____

Review

Use with pages 46–47.

Musical Matching

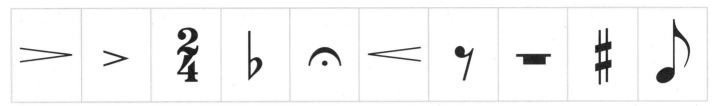

Draw each of the above signs in the correct squares below.
Draw each sign TWICE; once in the LEFT column and once in the RIGHT column.

☐	eighth rest	play next key to the left, whether black or white	☐
☐	fermata	rest for a whole measure of $\frac{2}{4}$, $\frac{3}{4}$, or $\frac{4}{4}$ time	☐
☐	eighth note	play the note louder	☐
☐	crescendo	hold the note longer than its value	☐
☐	flat	this note gets 1/2 count	☐
☐	time signature	play next key to the right, whether black or white	☐
☐	accent	gradually louder	☐
☐	diminuendo	rest for the value of an eighth note	☐
☐	sharp	there are 2 counts in each measure	☐
☐	whole rest	gradually softer	☐

SCORE 5 for each square correctly filled.
Perfect score = 100

YOUR SCORE: _____